THE BOY AIN'T RIGHT

by Hank Hill

**Created by
Mike Judge and Greg Daniels**

Art Director/Illustrator: John Rice

**Written by Jonathan Aibel,
Mike Allen, Glenn Berger,
Alan Cohen, John Collier,
Tim Croston, Greg Daniels,
Alan Freedland, Mike Judge,
Paul Lieberstein**

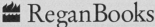
Oh Lord! I thought this was for *RonaldReaganBooks*.
I hope Judith Regan isn't the daughter who posed naked.

ReganBooks
An Imprint of HarperPerennial
A Division of HarperCollinsPublishers

HarperCollins books may be purchased for
educational, business, or sales
promotional use. For information please write:
Special Markets Department,
HarperCollins Publishers, Inc.,
10 East 53rd Street, New York, NY 10022

First Edition
ISBN: 0-06-095305-5
Designed by Charles Kreloff
Characters designed by Mike Judge
Contributing Artist: Bill Buchanan
Color: Michael Rice

Preface
by Bobby Hill

I can think of no better man to write, <u>The Boy Is Right</u> than my Dad, Hank Hill. My mom had told me he was working on a book about fathering, and I can't tell you how pleased I was when I overheard my dad tell his book guy the title. I am honored to be the "boy who is right" of this book.

Bobby "Robert" Hill
Arlen, Texas
Spring, 1998

What Is a Boy?

A boy starts out as a seed, grows into a root, and pretty soon he's a lawn. Just like a lawn, he needs mowing, edging, trimming, and watering...but not too much. You gotta be on the watch out for weeds, which can spring up at any time.

A boy is like a septic tank...you gotta watch what goes in there. Before you know it, his mind is swelled up with all kinds of garbage. If left untreated, you get a foul smell coming from the backyard.

A boy is a way to live out your dreams. You know, the ones that got cut short when he was born. He'll play for the Cowboys and own a propane company in the off-season. If your boy doesn't fulfill your dreams, there's always your boy's boy—the debt is passed down to him.

A boy is a chance to build your own Frankenstein, so to speak. You can show the world what life would be like if you were in charge of making people. Finally, you can create your own perfect human...until he starts thinking on his own.

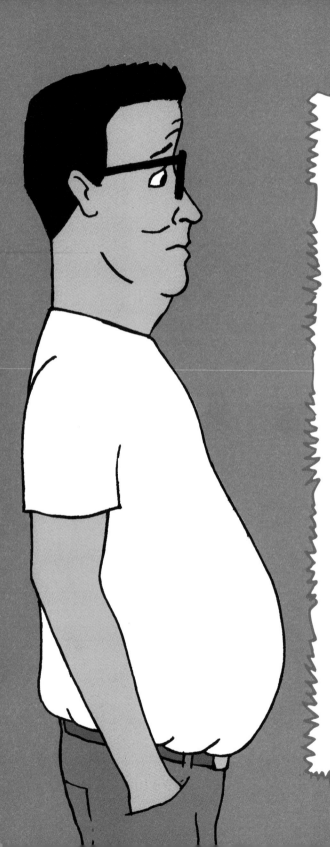

How to Prepare for Your Boy's Arrival

• Get rid of anything pink, unless it's bottled medicine. I need that.

• Baby proof your knife drawer with sternly written warnings: "Keep Out!" "Dangerous!"

• Get rid of pretty music and nursery rhymes. Just put on some Willie Nelson. He'll teach your boy about loving and losing at an early age.

• Prepare for your wife's postpartum depression by sound-proofing your garage.

• Start your boy off on the right foot. Decorate his room in current Dallas Cowboy fashion. You can find everything you need in the Dallas–Ft. Worth airport gift shop.

Questions about Your Boy's Delivery

"Should my boy be born in a hospital, or in the house?" This can't be a real question. The only appropriate place for the birth of a child is a hospital. Or a taxi cab on the way to the hospital. Or an elevator stuck between floors in a hospital.

"Should I hire a midwife? What is one anyways?" These are women who like to be around other women who are having babies. Yes, it's as weird as it sounds.

"Should I be my wife's 'coach' in the hospital?" Let's get one thing straight, coaching takes place on the field, not in a hospital. A man should not be in the same room as his wife and his soon-to-be boy. This is a special time for mother, child, and doctor.

"When should my boy get his first haircut?" I'd say about half an inch is a good time.

"Should I have sex with my wife while she's pregnant?" You hit the home run, why do you have to run around the bases again?

"Should I buy a playpen?" You should already have one. It's called a yard.

"How do I bond with my baby?" That's hippie talk. Just be his dad.

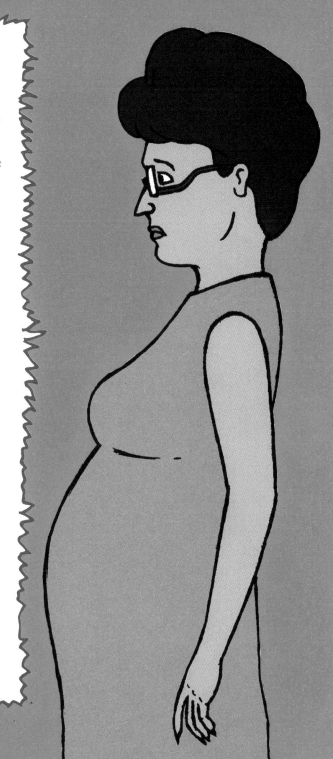

The Facts About Video Games

Here are a few reasons why video games are one of the biggest road blocks to your boy growing up right.

Physical. Constant pushing of small, tightly spaced buttons messes up the development of finger and wrist muscles. You might not see it now, but I guarantee that your boy's football spiral in a few years will not be a pretty sight.

Social. The boy who's got his head stuck in a video game umpteen hours a day isn't out there making friends or watching the television that he can remember so he has something in common with his new friends when he's older.

Family. Communal family activities, like dinner and breakfast, become a lot less communal when everyone's playing a video game.

Fathering. Try telling your boy what's what when all he's thinking of is how to get to the next level of Goofatron III. That's not a real name, it's just one I made up. But don't get any ideas about taking it, it's copyrighted.

Discipline. It used to be easy telling your boy he couldn't leave the house or watch TV. But how do you stop him from playing with a toy that isn't any bigger than a Band-Aid box? Even if you take it away, he could easily have a back-up unit.

Fighting the Trend

Don't despair, there is something you can do to save your kid. Make all of his toys yourself. I know this means you'll have less time for some important stuff, like making towel holders and instruction manual storage racks, but you'll be making something even more important, an upstanding, well-rounded youngster. Here are a few projects to get you started.

Baby Amuser. This basic learning attachment fits into any drill with 3/8 inch chuck. I'd start with a few nickels to amuse an infant, and work your way up to space shuttles for the older toddler.

Pull Cart. Easy to assemble, even more fun to drag around the house. Load it with slips that say things like "job," "family," "taxes," and you'll get your boy used to the notion of responsibility.

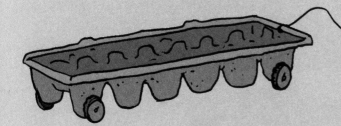

Fort. I remember building my first fort with nothing but some string, a few nails, twelve two-by-fours, five four-foot by eight-foot sheets of shearing-grade plywood, six redtails, and a palette of roofing shingles. If you live in a large, urban area, this could double as a safe room.

Slinky. Tired of sleeping on that old lumpy mattress? Open her up, pull out the rebel spring, and you've got a slinky for your boy. Tell him, "Santa came early this year."

Goofy Glasses. Take a couple of ping-pong balls, draw some bloodshot eyes on them, glue the balls on a rubber band, strap the rubber band on your boy's head and he's got those "crazy weird eyes." He'll think he lives in a toy store.

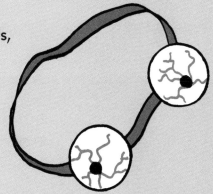

A Parent's Tool Chest

I know many fathers wonder, "Do I have what I need to properly raise my child." That's a question I always asked myself. So, I've gathered my thoughts about what a parent should have in his tool chest.

Four Hammers: This may sound crazy to you. I'm sure you're asking, "What could I possibly want more than three hammers for?" You have to remember that a hammer to an adult is a tool, but to a kid it is a favorite toy. Hours and hours of fun. But you obviously don't want a child to play with one of your good hammers. So a fourth comes in handy.

Leveler: If your child is anything like my Bobby, watching the little bubble move back and forth, up and down, is almost as much fun as a hammer.

One Nine-Foot Two-by-Four: If you thought the most fun anyone could have with blocks is playing with them, think again. Making them is the most fun anyone can have with blocks. Start with a two-by-four (a two-by-six will also do nicely), then run it through your table saw, there's really no wrong way to cut it, a block is a block. I found blocks one of the nice surprises in having a child.

A 180-Piece Ratchet Set: Sometimes when Bobby just couldn't be amused, I'd take out my ratchet set, open it up, and all those shiny little pieces would just mesmerize the boy, even the metric fittings.

Additional Tools: Of course, you'll need all the tools you can afford. You may not know why at first, but then you'll build him a tree house for his birthday or a new bed for his growth spurt, and you'll look out over all the tools you have, and that will make you happy.

Compassion and Understanding: Tool companies are not perfect. Sometimes one of their fine products can break if misused by a child. It is not fair to the company to get upset and toss around a lot of blame.

Bill's Advice on Single Fatherhood Adopting

Hank's said a lot of good things on fatherhood, and it sure sounds fun, don't it? Maybe you'd like to be a father like Hank. But you've got one small problem. You're a single man, divorced, with no hope of ever being married again. What do you do? Well, you don't have to steal a baby.

I'm here to tell you there's almost hope—it's called adoption. That's exactly how I plan on getting my family started again. And let me tell you, with my credentials, it's pretty much guaranteed that in no time I'll have a little child of my own.

Heimlich County Adoption Agency Application

1. Name
Bill William Sgt. William Dauterive

2. Why do you want to adopt?
I'm So God-awful lonely.

3. Why would you make a good father?
I was almost accepted into the Big Brothers program.
I'm appealing the decision.

4. Are you married?
I was and could be again someday. I joined a girl watcher's
club. And I hear women like men with babies, wouldn't
having one help me get married?

5. Would you be able to support a baby financially?
Two can live cheaper than one. As long as we both pull
our weight, I'm sure we can get by.

6. Would you mind listening to crying all day and night?
No, I'm used to it. But the neighbors complain about me.

7. Do you have the time for a child? Do you have an active social life?
Not a problem. Never has been. Never will be.

8. What parenting skills do you have?
The army taught me everything I know.

9. For women only. Do you believe in bottle feeding?
I'll drink beer out of a bottle or can. I'm not particular.

9A. Please, this is for women only. Do you believe in bottle, or breast feeding?
Both. I just happen to own one of those male breast bags.
The only thing I don't like is how it cuts me across the bust,
and the strap on my shoulders hurt.

10. Do you have anyone to vouch for your character as a potential parent?
I was hoping my child could do that.

11. Is there anything else you would want us to know?
I'm thinking about stealing this pen.

Ten Warning Signs that You're Not Ready to Be a Dad

1. Your predilection for strained peaches means there will be none left for the baby.

2. Your rampant toe fungus gives children nightmares.

3. Your rampant back hair gives children nightmares.

4. Your ex-wife took all the furniture in the divorce and you've been sitting on a stack of old phone books for the last six years.

5. Neighborhood teens use you for paintball target practice.

6. Your afternoon naps are twice as long as a child's.

7. Your penchant for breast milk means there will be none left for the baby.

8. Scattered cheese balls throughout your house could be a choking hazard to infant.

9. If given the choice between having a beer or going on a date, you would choose the former.

10. You've never been given the choice.

Ten More Warning Signs that You're Not Ready to Be a Dad

1. Your VCR has never played a G-rated movie.

2. Baby vomit would stain your tiger skin rug.

3. You don't have a safety fence around your hot tub.

4. A baby seat won't fit in your 1970 Dodge Charger Fastback.

5. The pharmacist can't understand what you're saying when you call in a prescription.

6. You'll have trouble finding a babysitter you haven't dated.

7. You still haven't bought the changing-table attachment for your Soloflex.

8. You have a hard time saying "I love you."

9. Your chrome and glass coffee table has sharp edges.

10. You already have a swing in your house, but it's not for a baby.

Unto Us a Little Child is Given

A CHRISTIAN BABY BOOK RECORD

I Bobby Hill

was born at head and shoulders, April 6, 11:37 pm.
chest and legs, April 7, 1:42 am.

at Arlen Memorial Hospital and
Burn Center

in the city of Arlen

I weighed 9 lbs 6 oz

My Height was 18"

My Mother's name is Peggy   My very

My Father's name is Hank   own footprint

A Family Album

We might have had more children
if it wasn't for Hank's narrow ~~urethra~~

My First Home

new composite roof (30 year warranty)

aluminum gutters and leaders

double pain storm proof windows

Solid brass door knocker

heated by 70 thousand BTU forced air unit!

A POEM FOR A BRAND NEW DAD

A tiny nose
A gentle bite
The sound of crying in the night.
Who'd have thought, this little guy
(Scarcely bigger than a pie)
Could be so good right from the start,
At winning his 'ol Daddy's heart.
It's what you get,
For all you do,
A shiny boy child!
Plump and new.
He looks at you, this tiny lad.
And seems to say, "I love you, Dad."

Dear Hank,
Ain't it the truth.
Love,
Peggy

Qualities My Parents Wanted Me to Develop

A good strong throwing arm

The ability to call an audible during a pressure situation

A love for Jesus and all mankind

To be a nice and considerate person when dealing with propane customers

To get a good job, work hard, and don't complain

Eating Charts

~~Breast fed until I was 3 months~~. Nobody's business!

3 months	Chocolate milk
4 months	Developed Fruit Pie cravings
5 months	First piece of steak – cut up small
7 months	First full steak
12 months	First time to Luly's
12 months, 1 day	Second time to Luly's

Baby Shower Momentos

Dale and Nancy Gribble gave a baby monitor scrambler.

John Redcorn gave a "spirit bag". (what a strange name for a diaper drawer sachet!)

Cotton gave Bobby his first gun (a baby sized Derringer.)

Bill gave Bobby baby booties.

Hank Hill's Interview Questions for a Prospective Babysitter

- Are you now, or have you ever been, a White House intern?

- In his second year as a Dallas Cowboy, not his rookie year, how many rushing touchdowns did Emmit Smith have?

- Do you drink American or Imported Beer? (Trick question, you're too young to drink.)

- On Saturday nights, Mrs. Hill and I like to stay out late, so will your parents be upset if I bring you back after 8 p.m.?

- Who was a better President—Abraham Lincoln or Ronald Reagan?

- If a little boy were choking on, let's say. a too-big hunk of fruit pie, do you know how to perform the Heimlich Maneuver?

- A follow-up question: If the choking victim was a pure-bred Georgia Bloodhound named Ladybird, do you know how to give mouth-to-mouth?

- Is any area of your body, other than your ears, pierced? (Yes or no will suffice, I don't wanna know where because you're already disqualified.)

- Do you know how to operate an electric stove? Well it won't do you any good because all you'll find here is propane.

- What does your boyfriend do for a living? (If you answered this question at all, you are disqualified because you have a boyfriend. Note: This applies to both male and female applicants.)

- In case of a torrential downpour, do you know how to tarp a lawn?

- If you are babysitting on a Sunday night, and my son asks if he can watch "Touched By An Angel," what is the appropriate punishment?

Being a Father Figure to Your Pet

In many ways, the American dog has never had it so good. He's living longer, eating better, and attendance at kennel shows is at an all-time high. Amidst all this success, however, most of us lose sight of one sad truth. The great majority of dogs never really get to know their biological fathers. Of course there are exceptions, such as my dog, Ladybird. She's a pure bred Georgia Bloodhound and was lucky enough to meet her legendary granddaddy —the dog who tracked down James Earl Ray (he was just carrying on a family tradition, his grand-daddy tracked down Alger Hiss). Unfortunately, not many dogs could tell the family stories Ladybird could tell if only she could talk. Most of them think a family tree is nothing more than a pee post. In my opinion, the lack of father figures for dogs is a time bomb waiting to go off. The only way to deal with this problem and make sure you don't have an unruly animal on your hands is to take up the slack yourself. Just like I'm a father to my human child Bobby, you have to become a father to your pet. I know this sounds like a lot of work, but remember—sometimes you can get almost as much satisfaction being a father to your pet as you can to your boy. And for you single fellows out there, it's a good place to start practicing.

Bobby vs. Ladybird

You know, the so-called experts say you should never compare your kids. But I can't help noticing the similarities between Bobby and Ladybird. I'll tell you whut...they both got the genius gene from their dad.

AGE 1	BOBBY	LADYBIRD
Drank out of the toilet	YES	YES
Paper trained within a year	NO	YES
Walked on hind legs	ALMOST	YES
Kicked leg when tummy was rubbed	YES	YES

AGE 2	BOBBY	LADYBIRD
Still struggled to walk on hind legs	YES	NO
Chewed on the furniture	YES	NO
Would give you the wet nose	YES	YES
Begged for table scraps	YES	YES
Marked territory	YES	NO

AGE 3	BOBBY	LADYBIRD
Learned to fetch	NO	YES
Had a favorite chewing sock	YES	YES
Learned to heel	ALMOST	YES

It's Not Your Fault Necessarily

Sometimes you work night and day on your boy and he still doesn't turn out right. That's because there's only so much you can do with the hand you're dealt. It's like customizing a car—you can play around with that manifold all you want, but it's still riding on the chassis of a `72 Impala. The good news is that, while there are hundreds of car models out there, there are only six basic types of man. Your job is to figure out which one your boy is, and then tweak him for maximum performance.

Beer Drinking Man

His brain regions are in proper proportion to each other, they're just a bit scrawny. Beer Drinking Man is not highly motivated to succeed but, with proper guidance, he's capable of such careers as middle-school principal, county supervisor, souvenir vendor, or army sergeant.

Twig Boy

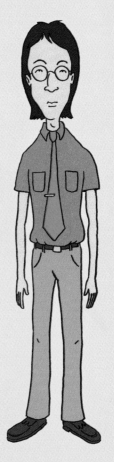

Unfortunately, the condition is genetic and is caused by him having excess language skills DNA, which has pushed the genes for manly self-reserve off of their normal spot on Twig Boy's Y-chromosome. The best you can push for here is a career in customer relations.

Figure Skating Man

This fellow is basically a hockey player with an overly developed "rage at father" region in his brain. All the same, I wouldn't give up on him yet. Once you get past the heartache, he's probably your best shot at Olympic gold.

Scientist Man

Marked by strong scio-spacial skills. Let him have them, the athletic sports region of his brain is almost non-existent.

Business Man

If his business is propane, this is about as good as it gets. Note his easy, confident stride, his fair dealing, his firm sweatless handshake. His brain's as balanced and efficient as a Northstar engine. Chances are, someone raised this fellow right.

Aikman

Not very common. In fact, there's a one in four billion chance of an Aikman being born every hundred thousand years. He's got it all, and the sacro-politeness region of his brain is so well-developed that you won't ever hear him crow about it. If you have one of these, there's only one thing you can do: hand him the ball.

Hank Hill Quiz

How to Tell if Your Boy Ain't Right

Most dads spend every waking moment wondering whether or not their boy is right. Take my quiz and find out if your boy is plumb and level.

1. You're watching a Cowboys game and your boy sees you crack open an ice-cold Alamo Beer. Does the boy:
a) Beg you for a sip of that ice-cold Alamo Beer?
b) Tell you that beer has empty calories and suggest a carrot-apple-ginger juice instead?
c) Ask you if you're going to be recycling that beer can?

2. You take your boy to a fancy restaurant because, I don't know, it's his birthday or something. What does the boy order?
a) The biggest steak on the menu.
b) The biggest steak on the menu, plus mac & cheese and some fries.
c) Something that comes with a sauce other than BBQ.

3. The boy announces that if and when he grows up, he intends to:
a) Sell propane and propane accessories.
b) Smash melons with a broomstick in front of a live, human audience.
c) Move to New York City, Los Angeles, San Francisco, or any other city outside of Texas.

4. You go into the boy's room, accidentally open his sock drawer, and by mistake thoroughly rummage through it. What do you find?
a) A picture from some gal that says on the back, "I like you, Bobby." And she's cute, not squirrel-like.
b) An old fruit pie that says on the back, "I like you, Bobby."
c) Lots of socks, mostly dirty ones.

5. When it comes to lawn and garden care, your boy prefers to use:

a) The John Deere 314-F Walk-Behind Tiller.
b) The John Deere 518-R Walk-Behind Tiller.
c) The John Deere 820-R Walk-Behind Tiller.

6. You and your boy are watching <u>True Grit</u>. Your boy mentions that John Wayne:

a) Rides a pretty, pretty horse.
b) Was the greatest movie actor who ever lived, with the exception of Ronald Reagan, who was also the greatest president who ever lived, with the exception of Lyndon Johnson.
c) Has nice, shapely legs.

7. The school bully takes a dislike to your boy and challenges him to a fight. What does your boy do?

a) Tries to reason with the bully. After all, every bully is a coward who will crumble if you just have the courage to stand up to him.
b) Throws a quick right cross followed by a series of left hooks.
c) Sticks two pencils in his nostrils and pretends he's a walrus. Before you know it, the boy's made a new friend.

SCORING

1. a-1 b-3 c-2   2. a-2 b-1 c-3   3. a-1 b-3 c-2   4. a-1 b-3 c-2
5. a-3 b-2 c-1   6. a-2 b-1 c-3   7. a-2 b-1 c-3

9 points or fewer: RIGHT
Congratulations! Your boy is right! He's obedient, likes steak and beer, enjoys propane and propane accessories. He's going to grow up to be just fine. Keep your eye on this guy—he's going places.

10-15 points: SORTA RIGHT
Well, it could be worse. When it comes to being right, your boy is on the ninety-yard line, and it's up to you to get him into the end zone. This calls for a very rigorous and disciplined training schedule. I'd recommend a strict regimen of praise tempered with occasional expressions of disappointment. And lots and lots of sit-ups.

16 points or more: AIN'T RIGHT
Sorry, but your boy ain't right. If it makes you feel any better, it's probably not your fault. It's his mother's.

How I Failed With Hank
by Cotton Hill

Let his momma raise him. She sissified that boy. - Didn't leave him in the woods and let the wolves do their job. - Let Hank drink water outta the faucet instead of a garden hose. That clean faucet water made him soft as a marshmeller. - Drove him to school in the pouring rain, when I shoulda made him walk. - Let his momma feed him warm food. - Let him marry outside the family. - Didn't ride Hank hard enough on shooting. - Bought him new shoes instead of letting his toes crunch in and curl naturally. - Didn't send him off to war. I shoulda started one. Vietnam woulda kept going if we had kept Nixon in office. - Hugged him once. I musta been drinking. Hank never tried after that. Next thing you know, I was buyin' glasses for his lazy eyes. - Let him sleep on a bed instead of the floor. - Shoulda forced Hank to become a man at the Hotel Arlen. I let him squirm outta it. If I could have just summoned his mannish desires.... - Married his mother. - Got him a dog when he was four. - Didn't get him a dog when he was two. - Let him come home a year early from military camp. - Fed him canned milk. - Gave him an allowance without making him earn it, once. - Showed him my war wounds at too young an age. - Didn't make him make his own football. - Didn't throw enough responsibility at him. - Didn't throw enough stuff at him. - Let him pick his own music after age sixteen. - Let him choose his own clothes at age seventeen. Forgot to enlist him at age seventeen. A lot went wrong at age seventeen. - Let him spit out his first mouthful of tobacco. Didn't force him to take a second one. - Listened to him talk. - Let him grow his hair all the way down to his ears. - Allowed them to fluoridate the water supply. - Didn't allow him to drink fluoridated water. - Under-chored him. - Didn't play him enough harmonica. - Towel dried him after baths—air drying was good enough for me. - Let the doctor spank him when he was born. (If you want something done right, do it yourself.) - Changed his diaper when it was full. Once. - Let him think I loved him. - Let him use training wheels on his bicycle until he was three. - Didn't pull all his baby teeth first chance I got. - Taught him how to talk. - Let Hank's momma "baby-proof" the house. - Bought medicine with "child-safety" caps. - Helped him with his homework. - Took his temperature the baby way. - Let him call me "Dad". - Bought him a car when he turned sixteen—and it had seatbelts. - Didn't make Hank memorize "Battle Hymn of the Republic" until he was two. - Never took Hank to the cock-fights. - Never made Hank stare long and hard at my shin scars. - Went to all of his high school football games, which left him with the mistaken impression that I would always be there for him. - Let him pet a cat. - Taught him to look both ways before crossing the street. - Took him on family vacations. (But never to Iwo Jima.) - Paid the ransom when he was kidnapped. - Rented *Debbie Does Dallas*. Couldn't get him to watch it. - Let his momma teach him how to shake hands. - Allowed him to eat with a knife and fork. - Taught him a five-punch combination instead of a six. - Taught him everything he knows; not everything *I* know. - Gave him his first beer at age five. Didn't make him finish it. - Let him see me kiss his momma. - Taught him thrill of victory...not agony of defeat. - Let him play football with a helmet. - Taught him how to shave using a safety razor. - Let him bring toilet paper when we went camping. - Let him go on his first date when he was sixteen...instead of making him go when he was eleven. - Let his momma give him a birthday card every year, whether he deserved it or not. - Made him practice the guitar until his fingers bled. Ruined the finish on my guitar. - Baited his hook the first time we went fishing. - Killed a rattlesnake that crawled into Hank's crib instead of letting the boy do it himself. - Cried at the wedding of Hank and Hank's wife. - Stayed with his momma too long. - Let him play with toys that didn't explode. - Didn't tape his mouth shut when he cried. - Let him go to school. - Went to his graduation. - Let him work in a gas station. - Didn't object when the minister gave me the chance. - Too nice to Hank's wife in front of him. - Didn't lock him in his room for long enough periods of time. - Let him spend way too much time with his momma. - Didn't fill out his draft card for him. - Let him stare at a mobile of animals instead of dead Nazzis. - Let him eat in the kitchen with his momma instead of in front of the TV. with me.- Let him hang out with Fatty. - Let him hang out with the skinny idiot. - The boy has no appreciation of strip clubs. He probably blames me for that. - Never paid off a guy to let him win at the cockfights. - Let him wear diapers. - Gave him a pistol instead of a shotgun for his first birthday. - Let his momma tell him I love you. - Not enough sausage in his pre-teen diet. - Let him run out on his first hooker. - Didn't force him to join the army. - Didn't stop him from marrying Hankís wife. - Waited until he was outta kindergarten to show him a bull mating a cow. - Didn't heckle him enough when he played baseball. - Never trained him by running him through an obstacle course—a live mine field. - Let him become a pump jockey at that gas station. - Never had his narrow uree-tee fixed. - Went to him once when he was crying in his crib. - Let him run out on his second hooker. - Never scared that idiot Gribble into running away; now the two of thems are friends. - Didn't kick his momma out of the house soon enough. - Didn't teach him the value of a Cadillac car. - Shoulda done less talking and more paddling. - Didn't tell him enough times the story of how the Japanese blew my shins off. - Let him wear glasses. - Didn't force him to join the army. - Let him hang around with losers. - Let Hank's wife work. - Let Hank's wife speak Spanish in front of him. - Let his trailer-trash niece live with him for free. - Knocked up Hank's momma.

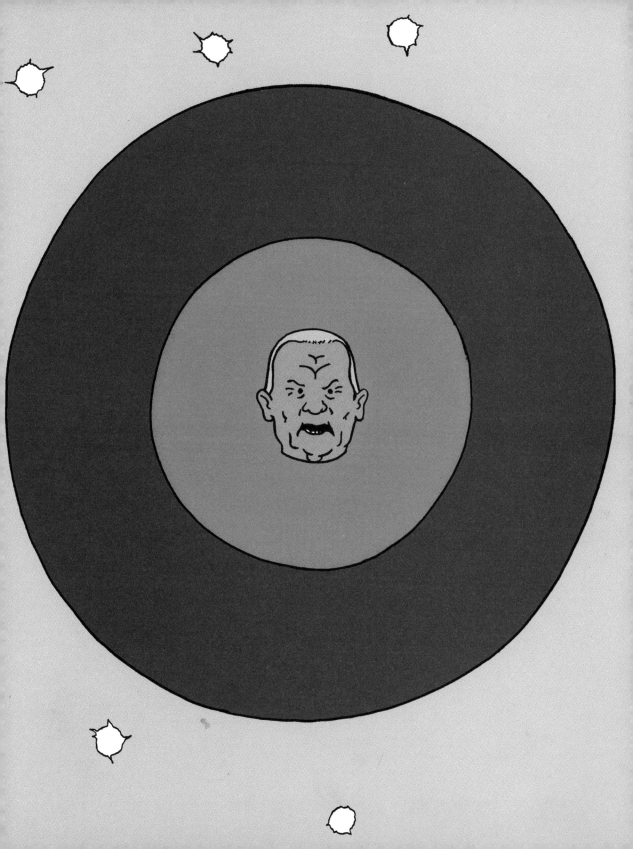

The First 21 Years:
A Developmental Guide

Age	By Hank Hill
Age 1	Attend first Dallas Cowboy football game.
Age 4	Learn words to "Star Spangled Banner."
Age 6	Learn principles of Reaganomics.
Age 10	Operate standing push-mower.
Age 11	Hit game-winning home run in Little League All-Star game.
Age 12	Kiss first girl. (Make sure girl's head is human not plastic.)
Age 12½	Go on first Deer Hunt. Kill first buck.
Age 15	Learn how to cook your own steak on propane grill.
Age 16	Get Texas State driver's license.
Age 17	Get Hank Hill license to operate riding mower.
Age 18	Begin stockboy job at Strickland Propane.
Age 21	Get married, lose virginity.

By Cotton Hill	**By Dale Gribble**
Attend first cockfight.	Destroy child's birth certificate.
Learn words to poem "There Once Was a Man from Nantucket."	Learn words to Second Amendment (Right to Bear Arms).
Learn to hot-wire neighbor's mini-bike.	Surgically remove child's fingerprints
"Birds and Bees" discussion. Also known as "watching a bull give it to a cow in a field."	Visit Roswell, New Mexico. Take first tour of captured alien space pod.
First barroom brawl.	Start smoking.
Witness first Texas State prison execution.	Last Halloween to wear G. Gordon Liddy costume.
Lose virginity.	Begin ingesting small doses of DDT to develop immunity for exterminator career/ biological weapons attack on U.S.
Join Army. Kill 50 men, become war hero.	Purchase first pairs of mirrored sunglasses (one for day, one for night).
Get married.	Get own set of keys to the bomb shelter.
Get account at local whorehouse..	Apply to colleges. Attend only if military draft is re-instated.
Buy first Cadillac car.	Start "borrowing" *Soldier of Fortune* magazine from local library.
Have affair, get divorced.	Find woman of your dreams, get married, remain faithful for life.

When Your Child Should See You Naked

As a father you have to make many difficult decisions. One of the most important decisions a father needs to make is deciding when and if you should let your children see you in the natural state.

For newborn sons, the best time would be the first few days of his life before his eyes are developed fully. The doctors tell me in the first few days baby boys' eyes have a hard time seeing much of anything and don't remember much of what they see anyway. From there on out the nudity should only come from your child and only during the changing of diapers or bathing, both of which are often best accomplished in the capable hands of your wife.

For daughters, who develop more rapidly than boys, all rules are off. Nudity has no place in your relationship. This applies also to other family members, especially those who are not blood related.

Look at the 60s. People got naked and we lost a war. Remember to just use common sense. If someone can see you, then you shouldn't be naked. Simple enough. If they can't see you, try to keep a towel on. We don't need another Vietnam.

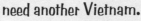

What to Do When Your Child Asks a Question

Maintaining the proper distance from your children is important. Many parts of your life, probably most parts, are really none of their business at all. But from time to time, your child may pry into your life. If you don't deal with these questions promptly and dismissively, you're asking for trouble.

Kids sure do ask a lot of questions. "Can I stay up late?" "Can I eat dessert first?" "Can I have a quarter?" Luckily most of these can be answered with a firm, "No." Every once in a while, though, your kid will slip in a really tough one, and you need to be prepared. What follows are some of these unanswerable questions and my suggested responses. Happy parenting and God bless.

Why is the sky blue?

Don't try to get into the science of this one, something about refracted sunlight and whatnot. The proper answer is, "'Cause that's one of the colors of the Dallas Cowboys uniform."

Where do babies come from?

With all the sex on the Internet these days, your kid will never believe your stories about the cabbage patch and the stork. So here's what you do—take away their internet access and tell them stories about the cabbage patch and the stork. And if, God forbid, they find out the truth on the street, or worse, the classroom, just tell them, " Keep your clothes on and your mouth shut until you're twenty-one." (Unless you've got a daughter, in which case, it's thirty-one.)

Is there a God?

In my experience, the best answer is, "Yes, and He's watching everything you do." Then—for the kicker—let your child leave the room, wait five minutes, and yell out, "He saw that!" Guaranteed to keep 'em behaved.

Why did Tom Landry retire?

I'm afraid there is no good answer to this one. Just hope they don't ask it right after you've tried to convince them there is a God.

What is the meaning of life?

To outlive the warranty on your hand tools.

How will I know when I'm in love?

Someday, you'll meet that special person, bring 'em home to meet your folks, I'll ask a series of questions, and make a few phone calls. In 2–3 business days, I'll let you know if you're in love.

Dad, why don't I have one of those?

Aaaahhh! Stop looking! Close your eyes! What are you doing?! No, don't touch it! You are much, much too young to have an arc welder of your own.

Some of these questions are brought on by yourself, from opening your mouth. Never share information about your day, other than, "I had a good day." Never volunteer that you had a good day without being asked.

If you should get a raise at work, you'll feel the need to go home that night and celebrate. Don't. Because if you let him know about a raise, the next question is how much—the exact kind of prying we want to avoid. Personally, I refuse all raises, that's the cleanest way.

On Saying, "I Love You"

The hardest decision in any father's life is when, if ever, to tell his child that he loves him. In some situations, it's highly inappropriate, while in other situations, it's just very inappropriate. What follows is a list of events at which you may be tempted to say, "I love you."

Birthday

No. For so many reasons: You say it once, you'll have to say it every year; all his friends are listening; and if there's a clown there, you don't want him to hear those words and get any ideas.

Bedtime

The problem with saying "I love you" when you put your son to bed is how you can gracefully get out of the room after saying it. If you turn your back on the boy and walk out, he could be laughing at you for all you know. If you try backing out of the room so you can keep your eyes on his face, you'll probably end up rear-ending the doorknob. Better just to say "Lights out" and run.

Scoring a Touchdown

This is probably the only appropriate moment to tell your son how much you love him. However, you may want to soften the blow a little by surrounding "I love you" with other phrases. For instance, "What a catch! I love you, son, for that great catch!" Or, "A game-winning touchdown! I love you, son, and so do your teammates!" But be careful, scoring a touchdown is itself a wonderful feeling. If you think saying, "I love you" will in any way detract from the moment, by all means, do not say it.

Deathbed

On the one hand, if you've never said the words "I love you" to your son, the moment before you die is probably your last chance. On the other hand, is that really how you want to be remembered?

Dale Gribble's Guide to Surviving the Public School System

Open up your eyes, concerned parent! Compare what your children look like when they start kindergarten to what they look like when they graduate high school. That's right, they look completely different. They are bigger, stronger, and are often wearing different clothes. All thanks to the public school system (hereafter referred to as The System), which wants you to believe that this transformation is perfectly normal. Which is what we do believe. But only because we learned it in biology class.

They call it an "education." I call it a "re-education." I also call it brainwashing, and so should you. That's right, the schools are brainwashing our children. Brain. Wash. Ing. You heard me. The schools are brainwashing our children. They are BRAINWASHING our children. They are—well, you get the point. Now, say it back. I'll say it with you. "The schools are brainwashing our children." Good. That's very good.

Why are the schools brainwashing our children? (And they are, believe me. They are. Believe me. Believe me.) The answer is simple—they want to keep you and your children from learning the REAL truths about the public school system.

• The school yearbook is nothing more than a highly sophisticated monitoring system (hereafter referred to as The System) that tracks the movements of every child in America alphabetically and by grade. Do you want the government to know your children's after-school activities, favorite song lyric, or where they hope to be in ten years? I don't. That's why my son has the runs every year on picture day. Your children should, too. (I suggest adding a squirt of dishwashing liquid to their breakfast cereal.)

• The schools want your children to believe that a good education leads to a good job, which leads to a good salary. Don't fall into that trap! Higher pay means higher taxes, which are channeled right back into the public school system. (Hereafter referred to as The Public Schools.) Never succeed. It will only take money out of your pocket. This philosophy has gotten me everything I have in life and it can do the same for you.

• If your child asks you for lunch money, you must never give him money printed after the year 1992, and you must make sure the coins you give him never include more than four dimes and two nickels if your quarter was made in the year 1957. This information will save your child's life.

PTA
MEETING
TONIGHT

• The schools teach reading, writing, and arithmetic, but they don't teach the subjects that will really matter after the coming apocalypse. Namely, etiquette and social dancing. They clutter our children's heads with utterly useless information like state capitals, leaving no room for important information like state populations.

• As a parent, never join the PTA at your child's school. Do they really think they can fool us with their fancy initials? Wake up people. Do I have to spell it out for you? P...T...A....Are you getting me now?

• They will tell you that drinking fountains are safe for your children. They will tell you that they have not poisoned the water and that it contains no chemicals specifically designed to render future generations docile and sterile. They are correct.

One final question: If our schools are so public, why are our teachers' home addresses and phone numbers so private?

Lies My Father Told Me That I'm Passing on to My Son

My tools are designed only to work for me. They are useless in your hands.

You don't look stupid in that baseball uniform.

It is impossible for me to increase your allowance given the economy.
(This is a slight re-wording of my father's lie, which stopped at "impossible.")

Your turtle is recuperating on a nice farm.

This is the happiest time of your life.

Nobody likes a smart-ass.

America won the Vietnam War.

Shirley Temple and Shirley Temple Black are the same person.

Don't touch that or you'll go blind. (One of the biggest lies of all—to my knowledge, a belt sander has never blinded anyone.)

I'm proud of you.

What Position Will Your Child Play in Life?

What position will your child play in life? If your son goes out for the wrong position, he won't do well, which could destroy his confidence and limit his ability to enjoy the game as an American. The good news is you don't have to take a stab in the dark. I've taken a quick look at the situation and a long look at football and have come up with a infant personality guide to football.

Won't share his toys . . . . Defensive Tackle

Stacks blocks with confidence . . . . Nose Tackle

Children with shifty eyes . . . . Wide Receiver

Late to potty train . . . . Defensive End

An insatiable appetite for fruit pies . . . . Center

The absolute perfect child . . . . Quarterback

Leaves toys all over room . . . . Cornerback

Completely unwilling to eat vegetables . . . . Linebacker

Can't get enough milk . . . . Fullback

Likes to picks out his own clothes . . . . Punter

Climbs out of the car-seat . . . . Roverback

Thumb-sucker . . . . Tight End

Wakes with frequent nightmares . . . . Free Safety

Handsome; likes to play with propane accessories . . . . Running Back

Late talker . . . . Offensive Tackle

Can stare at mobile for hours . . . . Defensive Back

Enjoys finger-painting . . . . Offensive Guard

Pulls on a girl's hair . . . . Strong Safety

Enjoys sitting in soiled diapers . . . . Kicker

Great Decisions I've Made

Sometimes it's important to take time out to pat yourself on the back, and that's what I'm doing now. I'm so proud of forcing Bobby to give up the clarinet that it's hard to even talk about.

Now, this may not seem like a big deal at first, but on second glance and every glance after that, it was a lifeshaping moment for my son. Here's how it worked:

Forcing Bobby to give up the clarinet:

Bobby never plays Bach and Mozart

Bobby turns on the radio and learns to appreciate classics of sixties, seventies, eighties

Bobby has extra time

Bobby has no choice but to turn to the football

Bobby is exposed to different kinds of plays, many of them ingenious

Bobby develops his creative side

Compare to the flip side and see how I saved my son:

If I had let Bobby play the clarinet:

Bobby is taught to push buttons and levers in a certain order while blowing

Bobby spends all his time sitting on his butt

Bobby is scolded by twig boy music teacher for not pushing exactly as told

Bobby is too busy hiding under funny band cap and misses out on the football games

Bobby loses creative part of his brain

Now, can I say that I had all this in mind when I took Bobby's clarinet away? Truth is, it was instinct. But that doesn't take away from the pride.

All Purpose Father-Son Talk

(Son/Boy/Son or Boy's name here), **I don't have to tell you how** (proud I am of/disappointed I am with/uncomfortable I am being in the same room with) **you. But your** (mom/teacher/coach) **thought we should have this little** (heart-to-heart/man-to-man/huddle)**, so here goes.** (clear throat/shuffle feet/punch son in arm) **There comes a time in every boy's life when he's got to** (put away the fruit pies and become a man/put away the fruit pies and show what he's really made of/just put away the fruit pies). **I remember when I was** (about your age, only more developed/screwing up just like you are now/captain of my Pop Warner football team), **my father told me something** (I've been trying to forget ever since/that really hurt my feelings/that I'm gonna throw back in your face now). **He said, "**(Son/Boy/Boy's name here)**,** (stop yer cryin', ya big cry-baby/stop yer cryin', or I'll really give you something to cry about/stop yer cryin', yer cryin' like a woman)**."** **So, there you go. If you ever have any other questions or just need someone to talk to,** (go ask your mother/go look on the internet/I'll be out mowing). **And remember, no matter what happens, I will always** (be like a father to/remember/have certain feelings...of fondness that, you know, a father and a son...Well, I think you get what I'm trying to say to) **you.**

Negotiating with Your Wife on How to Handle the Child

If you divide up which parent is in charge of certain parts of the child, you can avoid all talks on parenting. I suggest the following division of labor.

Father

Football

Baseball

Other sports

Mother

Clothes

Homework

Other school-related activities

Manners

Private talks

Day-to-day problems, as they come up.

Meals—breakfast, lunch, dinner, late-night snacks, fruit pies

Protecting from bullies

Bedtime Prayers

Listening to their hopes and dreams

Chuck E. Cheese

Birthing

Birthday parties

Weddings

Hoping for weddings

School plays

Daughters and daughter accessories

Making excuses for carpooling

Washing

Potty training

PTA meetings

Church

Personal grooming

Doctors

Emotional problems

Dandruff

Punishment

Etc.

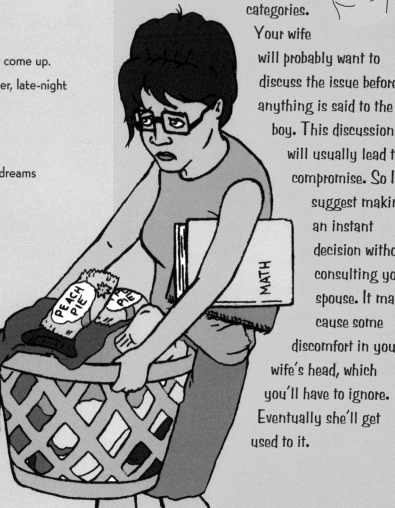

From time to time, however, there might be something that falls between the categories. Your wife will probably want to discuss the issue before anything is said to the boy. This discussion will usually lead to a compromise. So I suggest making an instant decision without consulting your spouse. It may cause some discomfort in your wife's head, which you'll have to ignore. Eventually she'll get used to it.

Nifty Notions

You've heard some fun ideas from Hank, and it sounds like dads have all the fun. Well, we moms can do kooky things, too! Peggy Hill can guarantee your children and their friends will love these!

• When your child gets an "A" on a test, do the NFL end-zone dance for your child and his friends!

• Put a smiley-face sticker on your boy's underwear.

• Part your eyebrows with a toothbrush. (A dry one of course, we don't want to get too crazy!)

• Draw a smiley face on your boy's finger!

• Stick a raisin in your child's food. He'll have a ball eating the "bug" in front of his friends.

• The next time you set the dinner table, go crazy! Put the fork on the right, knife and spoon on the left. Your child will think he's in opposite world! It's kooky!

• When your son brings his friends over, stand behind the front door, and growl in a deep voice, "This is the family dog. What's the password to get in?"

• Wear a "Coach Mom" T-shirt to your child's baseball game. Yell "good eye, good eye" loudly, so he sees you.

• Give your child a coupon for a "free hug in public."

• Put an "I love you" note signed by "The Phantom" in your child's lunchbox!

• Breathe on a spoon and stick it on your child's nose! (Safety Warning: Do not attempt this if either of you has a cold, or feels one coming on.)

• Stick a Band-Aid on your forehead. Pretend you're the "Very Organized Mom of Frankenstein." The neighborhood kids will love this.

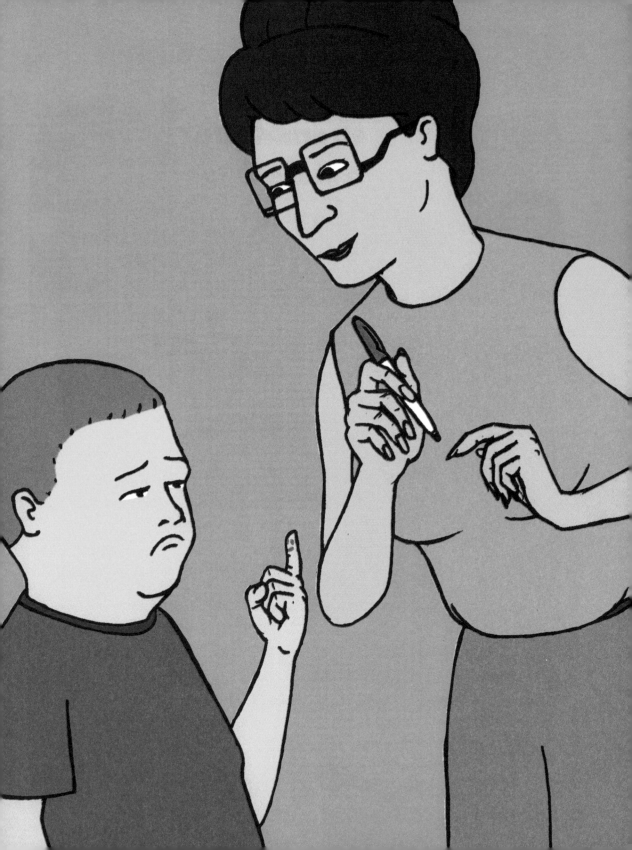

When Your Son Starts Dating

Sooner, or even better, later, it will come time for your boy to start dating. When he does, someone will have to chaperone him. Chaperoning should start with the first date and continue on until you are sure all of their sexual urges have been properly suppressed. And when your wife is busy, that unfortunate task falls to your niece. But she's unreliable, so you'll just have to do it yourself. And here's how:

• Whatever you choose for them to do, make sure it is something you enjoy, too. Invite her over to watch *Walker, Texas Ranger,* take her to a football practice or maybe to dinner at the local steakhouse.

• Don't let them both sit in the back seat. You're a chaperone, not a chauffeur. Keep the girl up front, where you can ask her questions about her father's employment and backyard grilling habits.

• For the first date, make sure to stay between the couple at all times. At this point it is best for them to avoid contact of any kind, including eye contact. For the second date...well, I really can't say. Bobby's never put me in that situation.

• Direct all conversation away from anything that might be considered flirtatious. Any sentences starting with "You look..." or "I like how you..." or "Do you wanna..." are not allowed and should be halted immediately. Try to steer the conversation towards good dating topics like beef or Dale Earnhardt.

• If you wind up in a malt shop, here's a simple rule of thumb: Two people, two straws, no exceptions.

• When the check arrives, let your boy pay. This will discourage him from wanting to go on any dates in the future.

• Avoid awkward goodbyes. When your truck stops in front of her house at the end of the date, tell your son to jump out and check the tire pressure. Then hustle his date into the house before they have a chance to realize what's going on. They'll thank you for this later.

John Redcorn

Eligible Bachelor, Eligible Father

Name: John Redcorn   **Age:** Forever Young

Height: 6'5"   **Weight:** 225 lbs.   **Eyes:** Caramel Brown

Occupation: New Age Healer   **Location:** Arlen, TX

Likes: Bringing my healing power to as many suffering women as possible, Classic Rock

Dislikes: Headaches, Negative people, Husbands changing plans at the last minute, Dust under beds, Rose bushes outside of bedroom windows

Thoughts on Fatherhood:

Often I wonder what it might be like to have a wife and child that I can call my own. I am comforted knowing that I am able to bring pleasure and happiness to so many of Arlen's families. I feel that through my healings, I have also been able to become an integral part of many families in Arlen. As for when I will settle down, well, only the eagle can bring flight to that answer.

Gettin' Away

We all have this problem on family vacations: How to keep your kid occupied in the bed of your truck. Opening the rear window is aero-dynamically unsound and would waste fuel, so talking is out of the question, thank God. I drilled a hole in the glass and rigged up a stick tied to a string with a ball on the end. I move the stick around and Bobby tries to catch the ball. This is also fun for me and my wife, so the whole family wins.

Materials: High-speed drill, fiberglass quarter-inch tubing about four feet long, and I recommend bailing twine and an old tennis ball, nothing fancy, just one the dog's done with.

Hank's Favorite Bedtime Story to Tell Bobby

First Lady and Presidential wife Hillary Rodham Clinton has often expressed the importance of reading to your child. Despite that, I still think it's a good idea. A good bedtime story will not only make a child's eyelids a little heavier, it will also teach them a valuable life lesson. That being said, if you tell these stories too many damn times you'll start to fall asleep yourself. That's why it's important to personalize the old classics, as I used to do when I told my son Bobby the story of "The Three Little Pigs."

Bobby this story is an American classic called "The Three Little Pigs." Once upon a time, there were these three fellas who lived in the make-believe town of Arlen. We'll call them Bill, Dale, and Boomhauer. And one day, they heard on Channel 84 Action Weather that a big, bad Twister was coming to town. So these three fellas each decided to build a house to keep them safe from the evil Twister. Now it used to be, Bobby, that a man could go down to his local hardware store or lumber yard and seek expert advice from qualified employees. But that's another story called "How Megalomart Ruined America."

Okay, so these three fellas went to the Megalomart to buy materials to build their houses. The first fella, Bill, a stout, somewhat lazy man, looked down Aisle Number One for his materials and then looked no further. Now Aisle Number One was the straw aisle, are you with me Bobby? Stay awake boy.

So Bill went home and built his house out of light and twiggy straw. Now just so you understand, the house weighed less than Bill. And part of the reason Bill was so happy to buy the straw was that the package said "Build a House In an Hour." Now it took Bill twice that long, but it still gave him plenty of time to sit back and stuff his face with a box of jelly doughnuts. There you go Bobby, now you're awake. The second pig, I mean fella, was a cheap man named Dale. The type of guy who'd step over a dollar to pick up a dime. He went to Aisle Two of the Megalo-mart and saw a big sign advertising "Half Off All Balsa Wood." Now I'm sure you know this Bobby, but balsa wood is among the thinnest of your woods. Thinner than this fella named Dale. So he built his house for approximately eleven dollars and fifty cents, plus an unreasonably high state sales tax. He was so proud of himself for saving a nickel, that he spent the rest of the afternoon taunting the Twister, daring it to huff and puff and blow his house down.

Now this last fella, the one named Boomhauer, was a well-read and well-spoken man. He had the good sense to consult an expert before building his house.

Now in most towns, you can do no better than to seek the advice of your local propane salesman. Which is exactly what Boomhauer did.

This smart and learned propane salesman advised Boomhauer to go

all the way to Aisle Fourteen, which was no small walk mind you, and to spend several times the amount the other two pigs spent. This was the brick aisle. And Bobby, lugging those bricks home in his friend's American-built pickup truck was no easy task, I tell you what. But after spending all day and all night laying bricks, Boomhauer had himself, well you guessed it, a brick house.

Now the weather gal at Channel 84 predicted the Twister would hit Arlen on the very next day. Five days later, it arrived. The Twister huffed and puffed and blew Bill's twiggy straw house down, and took all his beer.

Bill ran for cover to Dale's wooden house, but Dale wouldn't open the door for him, because he was convinced that Bill was either possessed by aliens or worse, a representative of the U.S. Government. But it wouldn't have helped Bill anyway because the Twister huffed and puffed and blew Dale's cheap wooden house down, leaving nothing but Dale, his wife Nancy, and her Native American headache healer.

Everyone ran to Boomhauer's brick house for safety, where Boomhauer was in his hot tub with several young ladies, uh, who were also seeking shelter, because why else would they be there in a story for a boy your age?

Alright boy, here's the big finish. When the Twister got to Boomhauer's house, it had grown to a level five, the biggest baddest Twister there is. The Twister huffed and puffed and shimmied and sham-mied, but it couldn't bring down that expertly built brick house. In the end everybody was saved. And the moral of the story is: Before you do anything, always ask a propane salesman for advice. Good night, son.

Great Fathers Throughout History
as compiled by Hank Hill

Ronald Reagan
The Gipper was probably the strongest man that ever lived. He was president when he was eighty years old; he survived an assassin's bullet; and he survived seeing his son become a ballet dancer, his daughter posing for Playboy, his other daughter writing a tell-all autobiography...on second thought, maybe he wasn't that good a father. On third thought, maybe it was all Nancy's fault.

Henry Ford
The father of the father of the F-150 pickup. It almost makes you forget the Ford Festiva.

Mr. Aikman
Anyone who could produce a son like Troy sure as hell did something right.

Bing Crosby
I can only imagine how lucky his children were to have that soothing baritone croon to them as they drifted off to sleep, comfortable in the safety of his arms.

Father Dowling
A crime fighting priest, now that's a nifty notion. Easily Tom Bosley's richest, most complex performance.

Dale Earnhardt's Dad
Unlike Jeff Gordon's dad, he realized that his son could be a champion with hard work, and not by having a racetrack given to him.

George Washington
The father of our country. Not much else is known about him.

Hank Williams
He may have been a hard-drinking, nasty sonofabitch, but he left us with some mighty fine music. It is a common misconception that he fathered Hank Williams Jr., who singlehandedly ruined Monday Night Football. Hank Jr. is, in point of fact, the son of Paul Williams, who is a fine singer in his own right and deeply ashamed of his son.

Tony Danza's Dad
Thank you for the gift of humor we can never repay.

MEMO

TO: All Strickland Propane Employees

FROM: Buck Strickland

RE: Lessons I've learned from bidness that you can apply to raising your children.

In the thirty years I've owned and operated Strickland Propane, I've come to realize that a lot of the principles I've learned from being a successful bidness man can also be applied to being a successful parent.

1) "Garbage In, Garbage Out."
   This applies to your child's diet. If you feed him nothing but fruits and vegetables, and no red meat, you'll get a wimpy child who's not strong enough to take out the garbage.

2) "Get 'em a Little Bit Pregnant."
   This is a lesson that applies if you have any young, attractive female domestic help. But it is a lesson that applies in the reverse. Don't get 'em a little bit pregnant—because there's no such thing. Otherwise, you'll be paying a little bit of child support for the rest of your life. Trust me on this one.

3) "Don't Dip Your Pen in Company Ink."
   I think I covered this with female domestic help up above.

4) "Never Be the First One to Name a Price."
   This is how you lose a negotiation, such as setting a kid's weekly allowance. Start negotiating with the tyke when he's five years old, and ask him how much he wants. To a five-year-old, a quarter's a lot of money.
   Then you give him a five percent or so Cost Of Living increase every year, more if a Democrat's in office. This'll help keep your fixed costs under control until the kid turns 18 and moves out.

DALE'S DEADBUG
555-DEDD

5) "Don't Take No for an Answer."
Strangely enough, this also applies to young, attractive female domestic help. As a side note to this one, I'd also advise you to keep a good lawyer on retainer.

6) "Keep Your Friends Close and Your Enemies Closer."
Let's be frank. If you've got more than one kid, that means you've got a favorite. He knows it, and his brother knows it. The brother will resent you for it and try to get back at you—anything from working in the butane business to going Menendez on your behind. So, keep him close and toss him a compliment every now and then. If things get desperate, tell him you love him.

7) "Leaner Is Meaner."
This has nothing to do with downsizing or firing one of your children (it happens). It has to do with your diet. Take it from a man who's had seven ticker-tacks, your doctor will try to put you on one of them low-fat Pritikin wheat germ diets, and you'll be meaner than a snake—in a bad way. You'll start snapping at people, chewing out your kids, and yelling at your wife—in a bad way. It almost cost me my fourth marriage, I'm not going to let it cost me my sixth. From where I'm sittin', fatter is happier. Now if you'll excuse me, I gotta grunt.

Dale's Stranger Dangers

"Do not accept a ride from a stranger." "Do not accept candy from a stranger." "Do not accept anal probes from a stranger." This advice is all well and good, but it barely scratches the surface. Below are some dangerous strangers you should teach your child to avoid.

Census Taker: This is the kind of stranger who asks intrusive personal questions, yet reveals nothing of himself, despite many hours of interrogation. Your child should hide from him. Or, if caught, should pretend to be an immigrant family of five.

Policeman: As an agent sworn to uphold the laws of our community, a policeman cannot be trusted. When your child sees a policeman, he should run as fast as he can to the nearest prison. This is the only place where a policeman isn't safe.

Mailman: He knows where you live! He has a key to your mailbox! His steering wheel is on the right! Need I say more? Perhaps, I need. He is a messenger, a patsy, and should be avoided or bitten.

Ice Cream Man: First he will cloud your child's mind with a dizzying array of frozen novelty desserts. Then, when you finally choose, say, a creamsicle, he will tell you he is all out. Then he will tell you that seven cents is not enough for a piece of double-bubble. Damn the ice cream man. Damn him.

Undercover FBI Agent: This stranger is one of the most difficult to identify. Things to teach your child to look for: Usually a grumpy, middle-aged man, who is one day from retirement, just bought a sailboat, and is on one last case with a hot-headed younger partner he doesn't get along with.

Pizza Delivery Guy: This top secret multi-lingual operative can get anywhere in under thirty minutes and carries less than twenty dollars in cash. That red insulated bag can contain anything and often does.

Supreme Court Justices: Learn their names, learn their faces. They are to be avoided at all costs. (Note: One of them can be trusted, but not as a lover.)

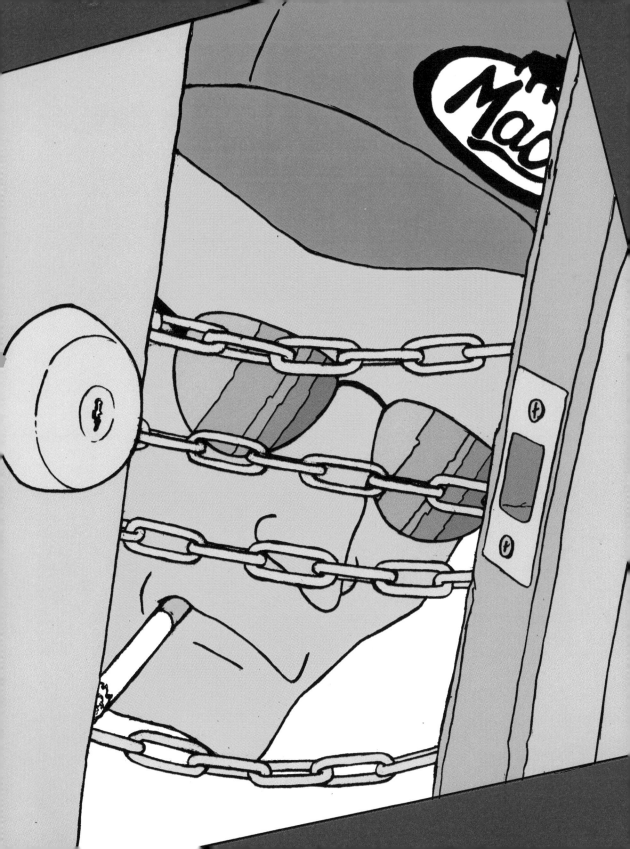

Cotton's Ways to Put Hair on Your Chest

Everything Hank has said is pure jackassery! He's sittin' on his boy like 100 pounds of dynamite, worrying if the powder is gonna get wet! It's a communistic way of thinkin'! Whether you're a boy, man, or woman...I'm gonna show you *How to Put Hair on Your Chest!*

• Swallow your chewin' tobacco! Don't cry about it, you'll get rid of it one way or the other! Spittin' it out is like spittin' out money!

• Stick a Band-Aid on your arm and rip it off! For no good reason! Keep stickin' and rippin' it until that thing runs out of gas! Then get another and start all over! That'll take hair off your arm, but it'll put hair on your chest!

• Open a soda bottle cap with your teeth! Don't use a fancy bottle opener! Use that eyetooth for somethin' useful! Chew! Chew damn ya'! Chew until that cap, or your tooth, breaks off!

• Shave your face with a dull blade! Save money by pushin' down harder! There's always some cut left in a blade! You just gotta find it!

• When you're liftin' somethin' heavy, bend over with straight legs and pick it up! Don't bend your knees like a sissy! Put all the weight on the small of your back! I wanna hear it pop! I can't do this one anymore 'cause I don't have any shins. But that's the price I paid for bein' a war hero!

• Turn all the lights off! Light a candle when you read! Make those eyes work! Don't sissify your eyes with glasses! Squint! Squint! Squint!

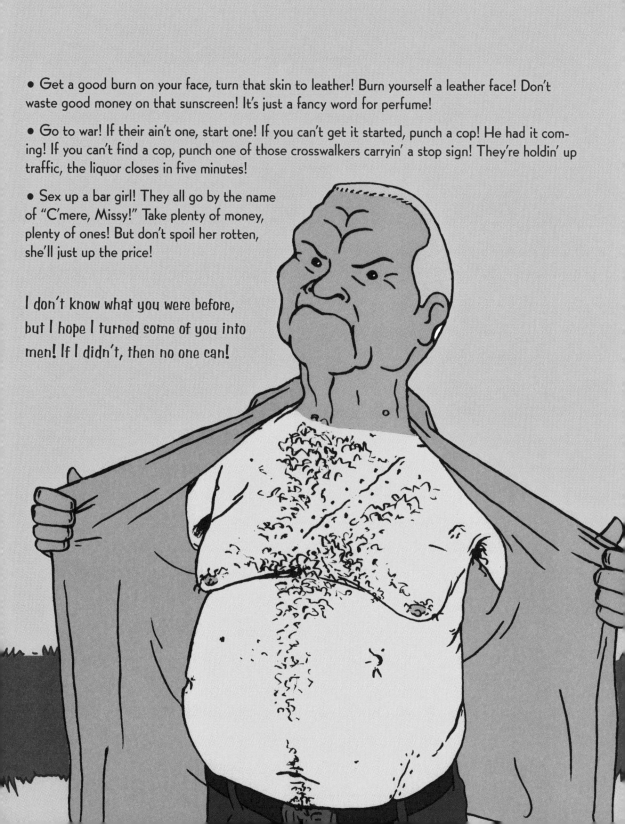

• Get a good burn on your face, turn that skin to leather! Burn yourself a leather face! Don't waste good money on that sunscreen! It's just a fancy word for perfume!

• Go to war! If their ain't one, start one! If you can't get it started, punch a cop! He had it coming! If you can't find a cop, punch one of those crosswalkers carryin' a stop sign! They're holdin' up traffic, the liquor closes in five minutes!

• Sex up a bar girl! They all go by the name of "C'mere, Missy!" Take plenty of money, plenty of ones! But don't spoil her rotten, she'll just up the price!

I don't know what you were before, but I hope I turned some of you into men! If I didn't, then no one can!

"Dear Hank..."
Advice from T.V.'s Favorite Dad

Dear Hank,
My three-year-old wants to drive my Honda ride-on mower with side-bagger attachment. My wife thinks he's too young and is worried about the sharp blades. I'm worried about my Honda ride-on mower with side-bagger attachment. What should I do?

Signed,
Worried in Wichita

Dear Mr. Wichita,
What the hell kind of father are you, anyway? A Honda?! A father's got to set an example for his child...and that means buying American. Before it's too late, get yourself a John Deere ride-on mower with side bagger attachment. As to your first question, I think three years old is a little young to be riding a real mower. Let him play with the Honda. Then, when he turns thirty, if he's shown enough skill and responsibility, he can use the John Deere. But only on the side lawn.

Regards,
Hank Hill

Dear Hank,
Every time I drink a beer, my boy asks for a sip. What should I do?

Signed,
Thirsty in Bangor

Dear Mr. Bangor,
First of all, you should be proud of your boy for asking instead of sneaking off and drinking beer behind your back. That's the way accidents happen. What if he drinks some kind of imported beer, or a lite beer, or, God forbid, a non-alcoholic beer. Next thing you know, he decides he doesn't like the taste and never drinks beer again. Mister, that will be on your conscience for the rest of your life. So do the right thing, and give the boy a sip of your beer. But not until he turns twenty-one. Heh-heh.

Regards,
Hank Hill

Dear Hank,
My child is getting picked on at school, how can I help him?

Signed,
Picked on in Pelham

Dear Mr. Pelham,
Rent every John Wayne movie you can get your hands on, stick your boy in front of the TV, and hope the Duke can fix him.

Regards,
Hank Hill

Dear Hank,
How tight should the bolts on the base of my toilet be?

Signed,
Screwy in St. Louis

Dear Mr. St. Louis,
The bolts should be hand-tightened. Anything more than that will crack the porcelain.

Regards,
Hank Hill

(Editor's note: Questions to "Ask Hank" should deal with issues of parenting. This question, however, was deemed important enough to merit a response. Hank Hill, editor.)

Dear Hank,
My wife and I just had a baby. How can we put the love back in our love life?

Signed,
Loveless in Louisiana

Dear Mr. Louisiana,
Rent every John Wayne movie you can get your hands on, stick your boy in front of the TV. Then go in your bedroom, close the door, and spend a romantic evening alone with a John Wayne movie. I recommend Donovan's Reef.

Regards.
Hank Hill

Dear Hank,
I have a problem. You see my son is a coward who never killed the Japanese in World War Two. Plus, he can't keep his woman under control. Oh, yeah...and he's got a narrow urethra. Should I love him? Just wondering.

Signed,
Ticked off in Texas

Dear Dad,
Please stop writing me. I have answered that question in a previous column.

Regards,
Hank Hill

Hank Hill's Guide to Movies Every Child Should and Should Not See

Should See:

1. Mr. Smith Goes to Washington—Reminds me of me for some reason.

2. Brian's Song—A touching story of friendship and loyalty. But I like it for the football scenes.

3. Caddyshack—A lot of people, myself included, like this movie for the comic genius of one Chevy Chase. But often overlooked is the true hero of the movie, the groundskeeper played by Bill Murray. Every child should see the extreme care he showed in mowing the fairways, and the way he manicured those putting greens. Right up until the end when he blew them up.

4. Leonard Part VI—Somehow I missed numbers 1-5 of this Bill Cosby comedy series, but if they're anything like the sixth, they are, to quote Artie Cavanaugh of WTEX here in town, "Funny!"

5. Wag the Dog—If you can get past the uninspired performances of long-time hacks Dustin Hoffman and Robert DeNiro, you will find a gem of an acting job by the great Willie Nelson, playing himself.

6. Beach Blanket Bingo—When your child is ready to see his or her first R-rated movie, this is it. I also own the soundtrack LP, but that's another list.

7. Red Asphalt—The most graphic and frightening driver's ed movie ever made.

8. Willard—Creepy fun for all ages, and always a pleasure to see that Ernest Borgnine fellow get what's coming to him.

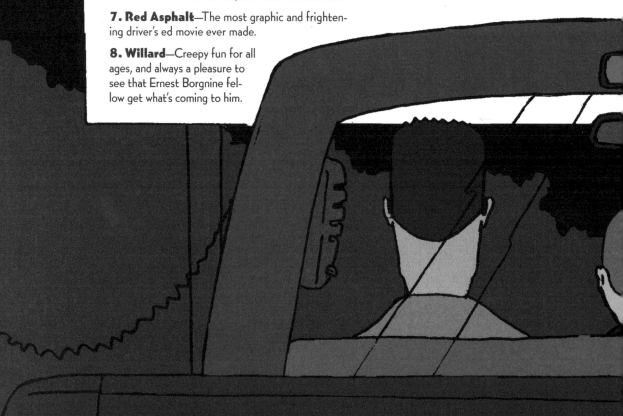

Should Not See:

1. Beavis and Butt-head Do America—I accidentally saw part of this on cable. That Tom Anderson fella, the guy who owns the camper, has a very annoying voice. It bothers me.

2. Klute—It involves prostitution. But more importantly, Jane Fonda is in it.

3. On Golden Pond—A sweet movie, but Jane Fonda's father is in it.

4. The Crying Game—Trust me, don't see it. Children or adults. You'll never forget the movie's shocking secret—the person crying is a man.

5. Footloose—A fella starts dancing and the town tries to outlaw it. Everybody roots for Kevin Bacon, but I'd side with the town on this one.

6. Black Sunday—John Frankenheimer's film about a terrorist who tries to crash the Goodyear blimp into a football stadium on Super Bowl Sunday. Includes one horrifying scene of charcoal grilling.

7. The English Patient—You don't have to be English to watch this film, but you sure as hell have to be patient.

8. The Sands of Iwo Jima—My dad made me see this one over four hundred times. That was before the day of the VCR. Sometimes we'd drive for days just to catch it on late-night TV.

9. Fried Green Tomatoes—Portrays all southerners as women, which half of us are not.

10. Sling Blade—An excellent movie, one of the finest depictions of a mentally-deficient man ever captured on film. However, the main character kills another man with a dull-edged mower blade. A smarter man would have used the self-sharpening blade from the John Deere SR-15. It is for this reason that I cannot recommend the movie.

Hank Hill's TV Rating System

Maybe you've noticed these little letters that are appearing in the corner of your TV screen. These are allegedly a new television ratings system. Well, I think I speak for the rest of America in saying that we don't understand it, and we're not paying attention to it.

With that in mind, I've developed my own TV ratings system. Peggy and I use it at the Hill house. Feel free to use it in your home.

TV-V = Vegetarian
Any show that discourages the consumption of red meat.

TV-GV = Good Violence
Your major sporting events, such as football and boxing.

TV-BV = Bad Violence
Any program where children talk back to their parents.

TV-CNV = Chuck Norris Violence
This is an acceptable form of violence because Chuck is only using it to apprehend bad guys.

TV-PM = Potty Mouth
There is no need for swearing on television. Except for the occasional "hell," "damn," or "ass." As in "I will kick your ass."

TV-L = Lesbian
To my knowledge this only applies to the Ellen DeGeneres show. So far.

TV-MA = Male Asses
This applies to shows like "NYPD Blue." Where Dennis Franz can drop his pants and show you his bare, hairy buttocks without any warning.

Kahn Souphanousinphone's Guide to Getting Your Child into the Proper University

- While still in mother's belly, read *Sun Tzu: Art of War* to fetus. Get ready for nursery school.

- Move to Texas—the competition is much dumber. I used to live in Anaheim, California. Too many smart kids.

- Save urine from age 3 doctor check-up. Just in case your kid go bad and need to take a drug test.

- Have child get after-school job. Learn how to save money. To use to bribe college admission counselor.

- Extracurricular activities. Need to set your child apart. Yearbook, debate team, yeah, they're fine, but you need something more. I plan to have my Connie swim English Channel. If she make it, she get into Harvard. If she doesn't, she not good enough to be my kid anyway.

- The more minority you are, the better chance you have of getting into university. For example, we put down that Connie is Burmese. They'll never check to find out that she's really Laotian.

- Many kids go to summer camp. It's very important to choose the right camp. I highly recommend Stanley Kaplan S.A.T. Preparation camp. For entire summer, starting at age nine. If not available in your area, move. You hick.

How to Tell a Child About the Death of a Non-Dog Pet

Telling your child about the death of a non-dog pet is one of the hardest things you'll ever have to do. (The hardest, of course, is dealing with the death of a dog, which is not really a pet but a member of the family. At that point, dealing with your own grief is your primary responsibility.)

When you find the pet hamster dead in his cage—Immediately remove the dead hamster and dispose of him. Then NEVER bring it up again. Wait for your child to force the issue with questions like, "Where's Fluffy?" or "What happened to Fluffy?" Please note: "Fluffy isn't in his cage and I don't know where he is," is not technically a question and therefore requires no response. When you can't put it off any longer, simply look your child straight in the eyes and say, "What hamster?"

When the pet turtle dies—Tell your children that it's possible the turtle has pulled its head, arms, legs, and tail inside its shell and they should keep watching until something pops back out. A child can only watch for so long before getting hungry. That's the advantage you have. Then, when the kids are out of the room, move the shell to another part of the terrarium. You can keep this up for years. Oh, and another tip—buy a sea turtle. They can live 'til 120. You'll save yourself a lot of grief.

When your kids find their goldfish floating belly-up in the tank—Tell them that they must have lucked out of and gotten one of the rare dividing goldfish and that it shouldn't be disturbed since it's probably in the process now. Then, when your child is asleep, replace the dead one with two new live ones of the same color. When your child wakes, he won't believe his luck.

When the pet snake dies—Tell them that God probably just needed a new belt and then treat yourself to the same.

When the cat dies—Just tell the kids the cat died. What's the big deal? It's not like it was a dog or anything.

If at any time your child feels the need to cry, tell them a fruit pie is in the oven and that tears sometimes make it take longer to cook. This has worked on other occasions with Bobby.

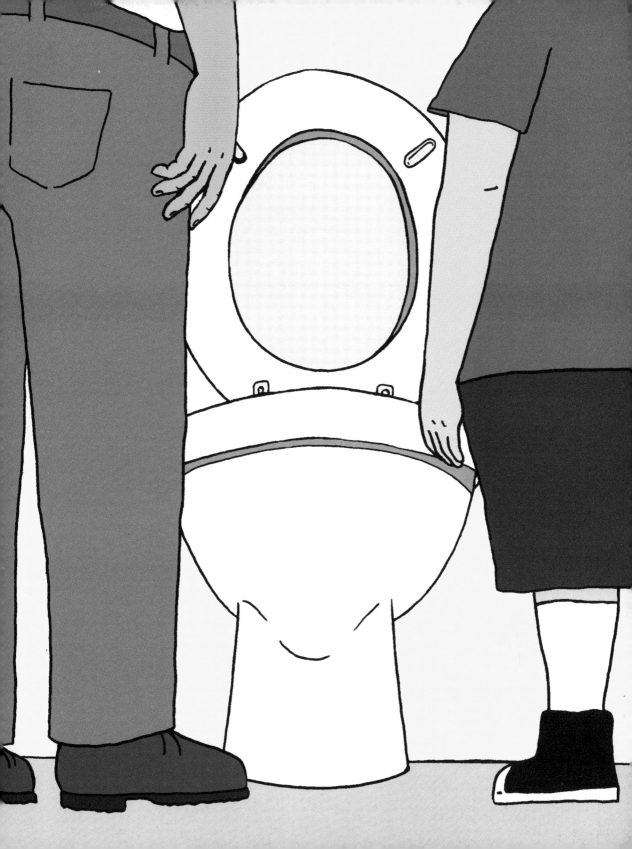

Dear Bobby,

By the time you read this, I will be dead. Perhaps from disease, perhaps run over by some driver who was let out on the streets by a Clinton-appointee judge, or, most likely, defending you and your mom from a gang of intruders. I know this is a difficult time for you and I want you to know it's okay to cry, so long as no one sees you doing it. You'll have your hands full taking care of your mother, helping her out around the house, and keeping the gentlemen callers from pestering her, but there are a few things I need you to do for me, too. First and foremost, please contact Willie Nelson and let him know my liver is his for the asking. Other than that, I want to be buried "as is," don't let the med school boys near me. Make sure I'm buried in the brown suit that I got for your high school graduation (as you get older, you'll learn that it never hurts to plan ahead). The suit is a poly blend and isn't likely to decay for a few hundred years, I think I'll rest a lot better knowing that.

Now for some advice I won't be around to give you.

1. Don't feel like you have to follow in my footsteps as a star running back when you get to high school. With your build you're probably more suited to play center.

2. Try to make it through college. I know two years seems like a long time of unnecessary extra school, but it would make your mother awfully proud.

3. As you enter your teens, you should be getting certain urges you're not accustomed to—to work harder, stand up straight and

learn the propane business. These are good urges, pay attention to them. Any other urges you might have are just these urges in disguise.

4. When in doubt, vote for the independent candidate.

5. Never try to cheat a three-prong plug into a two-prong outlet: God gave us grounding adapters for a reason.

6. Always mow with the grain.

7. Grilled meat generally tastes better if you get it to room temperature before cooking.

8. Don't pay attention to any other cooking tips.

9. If you like a girl, don't act too eager around her. Don't ask me why, but they always go for the guy with the bored grin. This changes after high school. Then they go for the guy with the job.

Well, that's about all I can think of right now. There's a chance I might have left something out, so at some point you'll probably need to find another male role model to explain stuff and teach you how to repair the new improved truck engines of the next millennium. I'd suggest Troy Aikman, he seems like the type who would respond to a good, heartfelt letter. If Troy's off playing football or something, you might try your grandfather. As a dad, he didn't do everything right, but a fifty or sixty percent average can be pretty good. Just ask Troy.

All best wishes,

Dad

Uncle Hank asked me to write a section about children's haircuts. And since I am a professional beauty-school student, I guess that makes sense. The following haircuts are some of my favorites for a young man.

Haircuts for

Crew Cut (also known as the Oops)

This is a classic cut, and one I'm really good at, 'cause all you do is shave. That's why I also call it the "Oops"—'cause if you're doing something else and you make a mistake (which I call an "Oops"), you just shave it all off.

"Not too short! It's a fine line between clean-cut and gang."

Comb-Over

If I make a really bad accident cutting hair—not the kind that needs bandages, just the kind that needs direct pressure—this is a good way to cover up the mistake. The boy can still go to school without anyone noticing something's wrong.

"Good Lord! He looks like Bill!"

Boys

Curly-Hair

I don't have many customers coming in with hair this curly, but I hear that the beauty school in South Arlen does this haircut a lot. I like it. It's the funkdoobiest. I'm also told that this style was much more popular during the 1970s, when it was worn by such celebrities as Gabe Kaplan, Art Garfunkle, and Bert Convy.

"What the hell is funkdoobiest? And who the hell is Gabe Kaplan?"

Punk

This look's not so popular anymore, but I was always a big Billy Idol fan. When I was a little girl, my mama took me to one of his concerts. We went backstage, and I sat there for an hour while mama went with Mr. Idol to his dressing room. I had a lot of time to just sit, thinking about how much I liked his hair.

"Thanks for the great story, Luanne."

Pony Tail

A lot of people don't know this, but the ponytail was named after the tail of a pony, which is what it looks like. And we all know how much boys love ponies!

"Ahh! Get it off of him! He looks French!"

This is why a boy should only have his hair cut by a barber.

Father's Day Gifts

Father's Day comes but once a year...so you really don't want to screw it up. Here's a handy little shopping list you can cut out and keep in your wallet... provided you've got a big enough wallet...which I do...so don't buy me another wallet this year.

Unwanted	Wanted
Cologne	WD-40 (I prefer to smell like a man, thank you very much.)
"World's #1 Dad" BBQ apron.	Plain, white BBQ apron. (The barbecue is no place for jokes.)
Collection of beers from around the world	Collection of beers from around America
Soccer's Greatest Moments video	Football's Funniest Bloopers video (Even the stupidest moment in football is better than the greatest moment in soccer.)
Snakeskin boots	Anything made from a cow, or that comes out of a cow. This is the greatest animal invented. If I was stuck on island with one person, I'd want it to be a cow.
A big hug, just to show that you love me	A nod from across the room that says you love me
Boxer shorts	For everyone to stop buying, touching, looking at, or thinking about my undergarments.
Gifts from the dog	A card from the dog is fine.
Dallas Cowboys Belt Buckle	Dallas Cowboys Superbowl Championship Belt Buckle
Surprises	Surprise me with anything from the above list.

Where's Bobby?

This is always a fun game. Try to pick out my boy in the following picture.

This Book is Dedicated...

To my father, Donald Aibel, and my stepfather, Shlomo Bar-Nissim. This isn't just your Father's Day gift. It's also your card.

To Sidney Freedland, who understands the fatherhood frustrations of raising his own Bobby Hill better than anyone.

To my father, Marvin Collier, who I'm sure will do his best to find something good to say about this book.

To my father, Robert Berger: Maybe this will make you love me.

To Paul "Peschy" Cohen, a great Dad, a great friend, and the inventor and worldwide patent holder of the Vail/Beaver Creek deep-powder spread-eagle face plant.

To my dad, Stan Lieberstein. I finished my book before you finished your book, ha ha. (Not counting your first book.)

To "Old Fuzzy", the Shetland Sheepdog who raised me from a pup.

To my father, Greg Croston. Your four years of tuition for an accounting degree have finally paid off. P.S. The bacon's still in my mouth.

To my father, Aaron Daniels. The screenwriter's leprechaun finally gets his due: My whole career, I have been exploiting your life, sense of humor and comic persona. Now as long as this book doesn't sell, my secret will still be safe.

To our daddy, Gary Rice, who taught us that being a man means working hard (even at a dead-end job), being honest (except at tax time), and drinking only the finest American beer: Pabst Blue Ribbon (or whatever's on sale).

Acknowledgments

For their invaluable conrtibution to King of the Hill, we would like to thank the following people:

Howard Klein, Michael Rotenberg, Richard Appel, Joe Boucher, Mark McJimsey, Cheryl Holliday, David Zuckerman, John Collier, Jon Vitti, Richard Raynis, Jonathan Aibel, Glenn Berger, Norm Hiscock, Alan Freedland, Alan Cohen, Paul Lieberstein, Jim Dauterive, Johhny Hardwick, John Altschuler, Dave Krinsky, Brad Isaacs, Joe Stillman, James Fino, Kenny Micka, Sharon Wong, Glenn Lucas, Kirk Benson, Robert Gaston, Melanie Middien, Lynda Lester, Dan Boland, Kevin Friedberg, Erica Clare, Jill Parker, Dan Fybel, Bart Coleman , Amy Wolfram, Tim Croston, Julie Mossberg, Rich Rinaldi, Kathy Najimi, Pamela Segall, Brittany Murphy, Stephen Root, Toby Huss, Lauren Tom, Ashley Gardner, Jonathan Joss, Chuck Mangione, Dave Herman, Jessica Jarret, Eric Friend, Louise Jaffe, Bobby Mackston, Ben Wilkens, Norm Macleod, Ping Warner, Ken Kobett, Ronny Cox, Terry Brown, Ari Emmanuel, Jill Anthony, Daniel Rappaport, Diane Gordon, Roger Neill, Lance Rubin, John O'Conner, The Refreshments, Gina Fattore, Brent Forrester, Brad Bird, Steve Barker, Sabrina Francis

Charlie Goldstein, Marci Proietto, Sandy Grushow, Gary Newman, Mindy Schulteis, David Robinson, Michael Hanel, Lianne Siegal, Sandra Ortiz, Anatole Klebanow, Rob Rieders, Sarah Goldstein, Carol Farhat, Steve Melnick, Peter Chernin, David Hill, Peter Roth, Rob Dwek, Lauren Corrao, Mike Darnell, Lance Taylor, Craig Erwich, Michael Clements, Roalnd McFarland, Kevin Spicer, Sharan Magunson, Shannon Ryan, George Greenberg, Suzanne Horenstein, Paul Mahoney, Cindy Hauser

Joel Adams, Ken Hayashi, Giovanni Moscardino, Martin Archer, Chuck Austen, Julius Wu, Gary Yap, Melinda Leasure, Swampy Marsh, Brenda Banks, Ken Becker, Jerry Brice, Robin Brigstocke, Eric Elder, David Filoni, Lynne Healy, James McDermott, Pete Mekis, Randi Neill, David Ray Preston, Jr., Polly Qin, Art Roman, David Salvador, Paul Scarlata, Jeff Stewart, David Swift, Yorland Tellez, Jan Inouye, Mac Torres, Dug Ward, Jason Yu, Phil Hayes, Cesar Magsombol, John Magness, Neil Ishimine, Phil Philipson, Ralph Delgado, Ernesto Escobar, Bill Flores, Chris Holt, Joseph Holt, Mark Linder, Chick Maiden, Cliff Vorhees, Paul Fetler, Debbie Mark, Belle Norman, Libby Reed, Cookie Tricarico, Kent Holiday, Acacia Caputo, Celeste Pustilnick, Jill Daniels, Adriana Galvez, Young Kim, Erv Capland, Phil Roman, David Pritchard, Lolee Aries, Jay Francis, Vonnie Batson, Jess Espanola, Tim Long, Majella Milne, Sib Torres, Kamoon Song, Don Barrozo, Lee Harting, Kurtis Kunsak, Louis Russell, Kathy Gilmore, Sarn In, Anne Osbourne, Erik Petraitis, Ralph Eusebio, David Singer, Stephanie Tuck, Damon Yoches, Elios Rios, Brian Hutchings, Jon Vein, Mari Provenzano, Amy Lynne Pucker, Greg Arsenault, Joan Thompson, Genny Sanchez, Richard Roman, Melissa Greer, Hyejoon Yun, Young Nam Park, Glen Kirkpatrick, Nikki Vanzo, Kris Yoon, Youn J. Shin, Paul Elliot, Scott Briggs, Choon Man Lee.

We would also like to give special thanks to Judith Regan, Joseph James Mills, Charles Kreloff, Lucy Hood, and everyone at ReganBooks and HarperCollins who helped make this book possible.

About the Author

Texan Hank Hill was born and raised in Texas and currently resides with his wife, son, and niece in Arlen, Texas. Hank's love of Texas is rivaled only by his love of propane. He is assistant manager of Strickland Propane, Heimlich County's second largest supplier of propane and propane accessories. Hank is the author of several other books, including *Strickland Propane: Employees' Manual*, *Strickland Propane: Guide to Employee Benefits*, and *Lady Bird Johnson: Wild Life, Wild Flowers* (with Lady Bird Johnson).

Conversion Kit

Editor's Note: This book was written to aid parents in raising boys. To make it applicable to raising girls, please make the following adjustments:

Page 6:	Change "dingy" to "whoo-hoo"; still don't touch it.
Page 17:	Same advice, only wait until age 15.
Page 36:	Change the word "knitting needle" to "barbecue tong". Ignore picture of Janet Reno.
Page 40:	Still use thermometer as instructed, but more carefully.
Page 49:	Turn page upside down.
Page 54:	Change "Hank Hill" to "Peggy Hill"; take everything with grain of salt.
Page 65:	Substitute "she" for "he" in all cases, except in paragraph two, where you should substitute "gals" for "lawyers".
Page 70:	Cotton Hill's advice: Change "Japanese machine gun" to "pepper spray".
Page 83:	Replace Willie Nelson song with Julio Iglesias song; cover ears.
Page 134:	Return book to publisher. There is no page 134.